Make Money Online Entrepreneur Series:

Book 7

Quick Income Formula Using Advanced Affiliate Marketing

KIP PIPER
http://www.kippiperbooks.com

YOUR FREE GIFT…

Want a free book?   Want access to more freebies and special offers through Amazon?

As a way of saying *thanks* for your purchase, I'm offering a free eBook that is only available to my customers.   Right now, you can get a copy of my book: *"28-Day Small Business Profit Plan: The Quick Start Guide for Business Success"*. This book is not sold anywhere else and can only be found on my website.

Plus, you will learn how to get instant notification whenever there is a new free book or special book bundles through Amazon.

Get the details at my website: **www.KipPiperBooks.com**

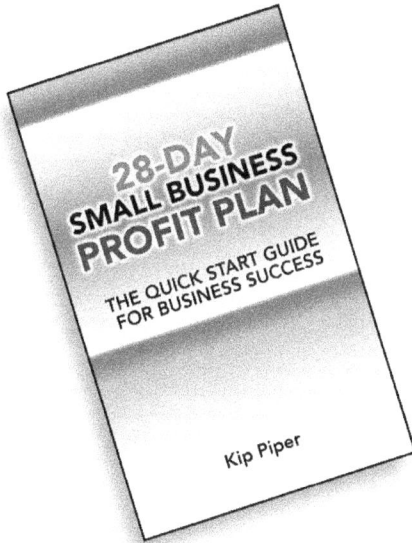

CONTENTS

Author's Note i

A Few Words From Kip 1

Introduction... 5

Online Business Success Core Values 7

Advanced Affiliate Marketing Metrics 11

The Gravity Metric... 15

Other ClickBank Metrics.. 19

Dollars Earned Per Sale... 21

Future Dollars 23

Total Dollars 25

Dollars Earned Per Referral... 27

Earnings Per Click.. 29

Affiliate Networks and the Metrics They Use 31

Putting Together Affiliate Offers.. 33

Bonus Materials 37

More Kindle Books by Kip Piper 38

One Last Thing… 39

AUTHOR'S NOTE

As you have probably experienced, the Internet and the websites on it are constantly changing. The information, examples, and screenshots presented in this book are accurate at the time of publication.

If you encounter any websites that have changed, please let me know by emailing me at: **kip@kippiperbooks.com**.

Remember, even though the website(s) may have changed, the principles, techniques and strategies in this book remain sound.

The links in this book are primarily affiliate links, which means if you purchase through the links, the price is the same to you and I receive a commission. This is the heart of affiliate marketing and entrepreneurship – which I am teaching you how to do with this book! I thank you in advance for using the affiliate links.

A FEW WORDS FROM KIP

Before I began teaching others how to blog and be successful with their online businesses, I wanted to be sure that I had something different to teach – strategies that are not easily found but can make a huge impact on success. The last thing I wanted to do is waste anyone's time. I wanted to offer something unique that would add both value and the potential for quick success for you.

Unknowingly, my research into online business success began in 1996 when I was first introduced to the concept of affiliate marketing. The potential for income excited me and I was quick to start experimenting with it. I joined Amazon.com and the few other affiliate programs available at the time. I added links on my website to products that related to my web design and Internet marketing business, with the purpose of offering quality resources to my website visitors and my clients. I encouraged and worked with my clients to include affiliate marketing in their overall online presence. I did this all in the hopes of adding to my income streams and eventually have affiliate marketing my dominant, if not sole, source of income.

But it did not come quickly, as others had promised or experienced. I totally, 100% believed in the concept of an online business and affiliate marketing (and still do), I understood the mechanics of setting up websites, creating products, and adding affiliate links, but I struggled with ranking my site high with the search engines and driving traffic to my site. Where were all the promised visitors who would buy what I offered or recommended so I could earn commissions?

Why were so many others achieving success? Why wasn't I experiencing the same success? Where was I going wrong?

I joined various mastermind groups. I purchased training programs from so-called "gurus". I bought books, read articles, watched videos, attended conference calls and webinars – I immersed myself in learning about blogging, affiliate marketing, and creating products.

The one most important thing I learned is that you need multiple websites, each focused on a different niche, to ensure a steady stream of income. "But," I asked, "if I can't get people to come to my first website, why should I spend more money and time creating websites that will not be visited either?" And each "guru" smiled nicely and said, "If you will upgrade your membership to our most expensive level, I'll tell you." But when I looked closely, I realized each "guru" was not living the life I wanted. In fact, most were working as hard or harder than I – with even less free time and income! They did not have the freedom of time and money that I wanted.

I didn't give up, though. I continued my search – knowing the one little "missing link" was out there.

One day I found it!

With this new knowledge, I knew without a doubt I could not only be personally successful with blogging, affiliate marketing and product creation, but now I could teach others those same strategies.

I realized that knowledge is what sets apart the training I offer – with this book and my other books which you can find at **http://www.kippiperbooks.com**.

This book is unique because it was written for *YOU*.

- YOU are someone who sees the potential in having an online business of affiliate marketing and product creation, but needs to know how to get started.
- YOU want practical strategies and advice that have already been tested and proven to work.
- YOU are ready for double-digit growth in sales.
- YOU are committed to following through with what you're about to learn.

This is why YOU are here.

Now please understand. Every piece of advice, strategy and practice has been tested on actual live blog, affiliate marketing and product websites – my own, my clients', and others. None of this is theory. You might then ask yourself, *ok, so how many blogs and affiliate websites has Kip done and what qualifies her as an "internet business expert"?* I think that's a great question. I wish more people questioned so called "experts" to see what qualifies them. As for me, I looked back on the last 15 years of stats and discovered that I have personally generated a 5-figure income in blogging, affiliate marketing and my own product sales – and that's just part-time!

If that's something you'd like to accomplish, you've selected the right book and series to begin with. I say "begin" because you'll soon discover that the learning process is a journey.

But don't worry! There's one more thing that qualifies me to lead you down this path – I'm just like you. It doesn't matter if you've never built a website or if you're already earning an income with blogging, affiliate marketing and your own product, and simply want to improve your sales. As you have already read, I've been wherever you are right now.

For anyone who reads this book and the entire *"Make Money Online Entrepreneur Series"*, and implements everything they learn, I can guarantee your business will move forward with more subscribers, sales and a stronger connection to your market. Like I said before, it doesn't matter if you've never built a website in your life or if you're already experienced, I've been there and can show you how to make blogging, affiliate marketing and product creation a successful income source.

But before we begin, I need you to do something. Connect with me on Facebook at:

http://www.facebook.com/TheRandomBlondeFanPage

I'd love to stay in touch and learn more about your journey.

You also are invited to check my website for more business books, and all of the books included in this *"Making Money Online Entrepreneur Series"*:

http://www.kippiperbooks.com

Thanks again for choosing to spend this time with me. Now let's get started!

"Done is better than Perfect!"

INTRODUCTION

This is Book 7 of the *"Make Money Online Entrepreneur Series": "Quick Income Formula Using Advanced Affiliate Marketing"*.

The entire series consists of more than 20 books, specifically written as an entire online business success training course.

Beginning in August 2013, I released one book a week, in the proper order to ensure success. If you follow the series from Book 1 to the end, one week per book, you will complete a 5+ month training course and master being an online entrepreneur! Of course, you can finish the series faster. Just make sure you fully complete the lessons in each book before moving on to the next. This way your success will be greater!

This series is carefully designed to give you every building block you need to build a successful online business. All of the guesswork is taken away, and by following this series, you will avoid most of the common mistakes made by new and even experienced online entrepreneurs. All is revealed – nothing is left out!

The beauty of this series is that you can pick up any book on whatever topic you need at this moment. Or you can purchase each book as it is released. Or ultimately, you can purchase the entire series in a bundle!

However you choose to use the information offered in this and the other books, you will be moving forward with intention and strategy for success in your business.

If at any time you have questions or desire personal one-on-one coaching for a particular topic, feel free to contact me at **kip@kippiperbooks.com**.

Here's to your online business success!

ONLINE BUSINESS SUCCESS CORE VALUES

Before we get started, it is important to understand, to be a successful online business entrepreneur, it is necessary that you stay focused on your business and have the core values that ensure that success. Here are the values that I have found to be essential to keeping focused and moving forward. These values will be at the beginning of every book of this *"Make Money Online Entrepreneur Series"*.

Be Passionate About Entrepreneurship

As it says, you need to be passionate about what you do and about being an entrepreneur. Being an entrepreneur will present the greatest challenges and the greatest joy you've ever experienced in the business world.

Commit 100% And GO FOR IT

One of the biggest things about being successful is being okay with putting yourself out there. Even if it's just a part-time business, commit 100% of yourself to the time you invest in your business. Commit to see it through and don't give up too soon. As the saying goes, "Don't give up before the miracle happens." Be patient and be persistent.

Build A Network of Support & influence

You must build a network of support and influence. This means building your Facebook community, building your Twitter community, and building your LinkedIn community. You must contribute to other people and help them be successful. By contributing to others and helping them be successful, you will become successful.

Get Comfortable with Being Uncomfortable

You're going to be doing a lot of things that you may or may not have done in the past. You can only grow when you're uncomfortable. When you're feeling comfortable and used to doing the things that you normally do, it's really difficult to grow, so you need to be comfortable with being uncomfortable see you can stretch and grow.

Consistent Growth & Improvement

It is important that you commit to consistent growth and improvement. We all need improvement especially if we are to grow and become successful, because staying up to date with the current tools and resources is essential. What helps you with consistent growth and continuing to improve is tracking your progress on irregular basis.

You also need to be okay with evaluating yourself and looking back at what you did and what you didn't do – without judgment. Simply observe and then recommit to the next step of growth and improvement.

80/20 Rule & Speed of Implementation

I'm sure you would've heard of the 80/20 rule (also known as Pareto's Rule) that 20% of what you do provides 80% of your success. So you need to understand that not everything you do is going to be perfect. Learn from it and move on. The quicker you get things done with the knowledge that you have, the more you'll be able to grow.

Flexible Persistence

Be persistent with everything that you do, and stay consistent with everything you do. The ones who experience the most success are the ones who are persistent in accomplishing their goals and are the most consistent in what they do. To be consistent, you must commit to regularly completing the tasks that ensure your success, whether those tasks occur daily, weekly, monthly, etc.

Surround Yourself With "A" Players

In business you deserve to surround yourself with the best and those who share your entrepreneurial spirit. You become like those you spend your time with. So choose carefully who you hang around with, so you are with those who think like you and make you stretch and reach higher.

The same goes for your employees. If you're going to outsource, you must select the best people who are competent and people you will enjoy working with. Avoid people who have negative attitudes. Surround yourself with those who embrace the concepts of small business success, entrepreneurship, and financial wealth.

Sell With Conviction

Be passionate about your product or service. Make sure you understand every aspect of it so that you can easily describe its features and benefits to your potential customers. If you have hesitations or doubts about your product, improve it so you don't have doubts.

Celebrate All Wins

Celebrate all victories! When you get that first sale, celebrate that first sale. Celebrate each new client. Celebrate each year of business success. Make sure you celebrate all wins. This is really important to maintain passion, momentum and to ensure success.

ADVANCED AFFILIATE MARKETING METRICS

This book is all about Advanced Affiliate Marketing.

As you know by now, affiliate marketing is the quickest and easiest to make money in the Internet marketing business. Why it's so quick and easy is that you don't have to create a product, you don't have to fill orders, you don't have any customer service issues – that's why affiliate marketing can be so great. Another reason affiliate marketing is so powerful is it helps you monetize your list in ways you couldn't otherwise generate income.

In other words, even if you have your own product, it's important to also promote affiliate products because not everyone on your list will resonate with you. They will want to hear from other people or may want to see other offers that they'll respond to in a better fashion. They may not buy from you but you do want to generate income from them as they come across your list.

This chapter is an overview of Advanced Affiliate Marketing Metrics. Then in the following chapters we will go into detail the metrics and numbers that you want to look at in trying to determine a good affiliate offer from a bad affiliate offer, a good offer from a decent offer, etc. It's important that you be able to quickly analyze and identify good affiliate offers, and of course, how to promote them.

Over the course of this book, we will be exploring metrics such as EPC, Gravity, and ClickBank metrics. We are also going to cover how to put different affiliate marketing offers together, how to build complex affiliate marketing offers, and some advanced promotion strategies so you can generate the most dollars per sale.

EPC = Earnings Per Click

In my opinion EPC, or Earnings Per Click, is the important metric to look at when choosing an affiliate offer.

What is EPC? Earnings Per Click is simply the total dollar amount sold divided by the number of times that link is clicked. In other words, anytime someone clicks a link to go to a sales page or to go to an offer page, what are the Earnings Per Click.

Earnings Per Click is a really good metric because it takes into account a lot of different factors. When you look at Gravity and at other different metrics, on the surface these metrics might indicate a really good promotion.

As an example, let's say there is a promotion that generated $200,000 in sales. This could be construed as a really good promotion. However, 2 million people clicked on the link and looked at this offer. When you think of 2 million people looking at the offer and having only 200,000 in sales, that's only $.10 Earnings Per Click. This is really a horrible sales metric!

So the Earnings Per Click really gives you a good idea about how well your traffic is going to convert and how much each visitor is worth to you.

So looking at the Earnings Per Click you ask yourself, if you get people to click on your email link to an affiliate offer, what can you expect to earn?

Remember, you don't care about the total number of visitors – you want to know how much you're going to make from every person that you sent to that affiliate offer.

When looking at EPC, if an offer has never sold and has an EPC of zero versus an offer that has an EPC of three dollars, which one is more likely to convert better? The one with the higher EPC.

If you were creating your own product, this is also important to keep in mind because you should always be looking for ways to increase your EPC. These are the things that good affiliate marketers look at what they're looking for offers to promote. As you create and start selling your own product, one of the things you always want to improve is that Earnings Per Click metric.

Different Affiliate Networks Use Different Metrics

Different affiliate networks are going to look at different metrics.

ClickBank, which is a very large affiliate network in the digital products space, uses Gravity as their main metric. Gravity is a metric that causes lots of discussion and interpretation. We'll discuss Gravity in more detail later in this book.

Commission Junction (CJ) uses EPC as their primary metric.

ClickBooth also uses EPC their main metric.

So above are a few examples of affiliate networks and the metrics that they use to determine and differentiate offers, such as, what's selling, what's not selling, etc. we will be discussing these in greater detail. We are talking about affiliate marketing metrics as part of advanced affiliate marketing because ultimately these metrics help you identify and differentiate between the multitude of offers that are out there.

THE GRAVITY METRIC

This chapter on Advanced Affiliate Marketing is about and advanced affiliate marketing metric known as "Gravity".

The Gravity metric is specific to the ClickBank affiliate network. ClickBank is the largest digital product affiliate network on the Internet today. Gravity is what ClickBank uses to help you identify good affiliate offers to promote.

What is Gravity?

Gravity is the number of affiliates who have made a sale in the past eight weeks. The sum is weighted over the eight-week period.

In other words, a product is going to have a higher Gravity if 10 people have made sales in the most recent week versus if 10 people had made sales eight weeks ago. The sales eight weeks ago have weight in determining gravity, however they will not have as high a weight as if it is a recent sale.

Gravity ≠ Sales

It's very important to understand that Gravity does **not** equal Sales.

Gravity is **not** a direct reflection of sales. If a product had only one affiliate make sales in the past week, but that affiliate made 1,000 sales, it would only have a Gravity of "1".

But if you have 1,000 affiliates make one sale each, then the Gravity would be "1,000".

Gravity is based on the number of individual affiliates that makes sales, not necessarily the total volume of sales.

Is Gravity good or is Gravity bad or is Gravity indifferent?

It's important to understand what Gravity is and take it for what it is, and not make it something that it is not.

Gravity will help you identify how many individual people are making sales. That's a pretty good metric! Why? Because it means a lot of people are promoting the affiliate offer, but more importantly, they are actually converting and making sales.

So let's look at Gravity a little bit deeper.

Can high Gravity be bad?

This is a question that I get a lot. Yes, it can be bad – because the higher the Gravity, the higher the competition.

So is a lower Gravity better?

No, a lower Gravity generally means that the product's affiliates aren't making any sales. It can also mean that not very many affiliates are making sales.

So if high Gravity is bad and low Gravity is bad...

Is there a sweet spot?

Simply, there is no clearly identifiable sweet spot. Gravity is a metric that you shouldn't follow too closely.

If Gravity is super high, that means that a lot different people are making sales.

For example, someone is doing a new product launch and they're running all of their sales through ClickBank. This means that they are promoting it very heavily through email, and they already have a lot of affiliates on board. If that launch is currently going on when you're looking at this affiliate offer, then the Gravity will probably be super high. It is artificially inflated.

On the other hand, if there is a lot of buzz and a lot of people are promoting the new product, it's probably converting well.

Another consideration about high Gravity versus low Gravity, I would much rather look at a higher Gravity offer than a "0" Gravity offer. While a high Gravity offer has more competition and more people are promoting it, I'd rather be promoting it because of proven conversion and sales rather than something that is not selling at all and has a "0" Gravity.

When we are talking about marketing online, there *are* competitive niches and competitive products. That's okay! Because if they are competitive and they are selling, what does that mean? That they are selling!

There are sales happening! Competition is not always a bad thing. So don't be scared away from competition.

When it comes to Gravity, it indicates how many affiliates are making sales with that product over an eight-week period.

KIP PIPER

OTHER CLICKBANK METRICS

ClickBank also uses other important metrics when they're trying to determine the quality of an offer. Gravity is only one common metric. Now we will take a look at a few others.

Dollars Earned Per Sale

This is the dollar amount earned for every sale that's made that particular product.

Future Dollars

This is important when you're taking into account offers that have some sort of continuity or subscription-based website or reoccurring payments.

Total Dollars

This is a combination of all the different ways you could be compensated as an affiliate. In other words, this is the overall total dollars earned per referral.

Let's look at these metrics in detail.

DOLLARS EARNED PER SALE

This is pretty straightforward. Dollars Earned Per Sale is the average net amount earned per affiliate per referred sale. This number is impacted by refunds, chargebacks, and sales tax.

For example, let's say the product sells for $100. The referral amount or commission is 50%. So if the commission is 50% and the total sale is $100, the actual commission payment is not going to be $50. That is because there are different costs that go into they Dollars Earned Per Sale. There are fees that ClickBank charges, there may be a sales tax depending on the type of product, etc. after all of the different costs are considered, the payment you actually receive will probably be about $44-$45.

So Dollars Earned Per Sale is the actual dollar amount earned her sale that you can expect to receive as payment.

FUTURE DOLLARS

Future Dollars refers to products that have a rebill or recurring revenue. In other words, it's the average total rebill revenue earned by the affiliate due to sales from a site. Generally this equates to the average sum of rebills.

What's important with continuity, or any sort of product that has a recurring payment or has a membership portion to the product, is knowing the "Stick Rate". The Stick Rate simply is the length of time which somebody is going to "stick" and continue to use the product.

For example, if a product has a payment of $100 per month and the average user stays for six months, what are the total future dollars? If this product has a 50% commission, then the formula is:

50% x (6 x $100) = $300 - fees and other costs = approximately $280

Future Dollars is important because some products you promote may be one-time sales and others may be recurring. Future Dollars allows you a better idea when comparing similar products on what is the monetary total benefit per sale you're going to make.

For instance, you sell a $100 product with a 50% commission. In addition, you sell a $30 product with a 50% continuity commission, but the average customer stays for a year. Which product is going to pay you more in Future Dollars?

You are going to receive more in Future Dollars from selling the continuity product than selling just that $100 product and making that $50 once. Here is the formula for the continuity product:

50% x (12 x $30) = $180 Future Dollars

Future Dollars allows us to compare similar products where one product offers a one-time commission and the second product offers a continuity commission.

TOTAL DOLLARS

Total Dollars is a combination of future dollars and upfront sales.

Initial Sales + Rebills ÷ # of Initial Sales = Total Dollars

Essentially, Total Dollars is the sum of all initial sales and rebills divided by the number of initial sales. It is the average total dollar per sale (per customer), including all rebills that may come from that sale.

Total Dollars is the real number that you want to be concerned with. This tells us how much you can expect from a sale that you're going to make. It's not just about the first sale but what is the total dollar amount that referred customer is worth to you as an affiliate marketer.

DOLLARS EARNED PER REFERRAL

Dollars Earned Per Referral is the average percentage commission earned per affiliate per referred sale. This number should only vary if the vendor has changed their commission percentage over time.

Remember, just because a ClickBank offer has a 50% commission today, that does not mean that it was 50% yesterday nor does it mean it will be 50% tomorrow. A product owner can change their payout commission over time.

The Dollars Earned Per Referral metric allows you to see what the average payout is per referred sale – not just for the last day, last two days or week, but over time.

* * * * * *

This finishes our discussion of the other important ClickBank metrics. In the end when you are thinking about these metrics in terms of ClickBank, which are essentially the Initial Sale, the Total Dollars per sale and Future Dollars, the metrics help you compare apples to apples when you're looking at different ClickBank offers to promote.

In my opinion, the most important metric is Total Dollars. You want to know the total dollar amount that you can expect as an affiliate promoting a ClickBank product.

Remember, if you take the total dollar amount of a one-time product sale or take the total dollar amount of a continuity product, then you can compare the two to determine what the average income is going to be for you as an affiliate. After all, the income is what you are concerned about.

EARNINGS PER CLICK

Another great affiliate marketing metric is EPC or Earnings Per Click. EPC is one of the most complete metrics for affiliate marketing – or any online marketing for that matter. It is also important when you are monitoring your own sales funnel once you create your own product. EPC is very widely respected as the most accurate reflection of the effectiveness of a particular offer.

The formula for EPC (or Earnings Per Click) is really easy to understand and use. EPC equals the Total Dollars Made divided by the number of Unique Clicks to the sales page or to the offer page.

EPC = Total Dollars Made ÷ # of Unique Clicks

A Unique Click is a click that is unique to only one computer. If the same visitor clicks your link twice, it's only counted once.

Earnings Per Click is a great metric for affiliate offers, because you as the promoter use EPC to determine the effectiveness of the offer to your list.

For example, you have 100 people that click your link to go to a sales page and the offer is selling at $100. Let's say 10 people buy the product. If 10 people buy, that's a total dollar amount of $1,000. 100 people clicked that link and you generated $1,000 in sales, so your Earnings Per Click is $10. Here is the formula:

$1,000 total sales ÷ 100 clicks = $10 EPC

Is a higher EPC better?

Yes, indeed! When the EPC is higher, this means the offer is converting well.

What is a good EPC?

Commonly accepted in the affiliate marketing industry is $1-$6 per click. Obviously, if it is more than that – if you're looking at $10, $15, or higher per click – that is a fabulous offer! But anywhere between $1-$6 per click is an offer you want to look at.

If the EPC is less than $1, unless it's a product that is *really* good for your list, you probably want to stay away from it. If it's more than $6, you definitely want to look into it. Honestly, you won't see many offers at more than $6 EPC.

Counting Chickens Before They Hatch

It's easy with EPC to count your sales based on your clicks. But you must be careful not to get ahead of yourself. There are a lot of factors that go into the reasons why some offers convert and others don't to a particular list.

The biggest thing you want to think about, as it pertains to EPC, is your list may respond differently to an offer than another list. So when you're looking at the metric for EPC, you have to understand that, if your list is better or more responsive to you then other people who are promoting that product, you can expect a higher EPC because your list will convert better.

One of the important things about Advanced Affiliate Marketing in general when we are talking about generating affiliate sales, many people fail to take into account that you as the affiliate marketer have a lot to do with the effectiveness of every offer. Your ability to pre-sell or help facilitate the offer before your prospects actually get to the offer page of the product you are promoting will have a huge impact on your overall EPC and your overall conversions.

So always keep that in mind that you can greatly affect the EPC of any offer you promote by doing as much pre-selling as possible.

AFFILIATE NETWORKS
AND THE METRICS THEY USE

In this chapter we're going to draw some conclusions about the different affiliate networks and the metrics they use.

First, metrics can be good. They are a great starting point for choosing the offers you're going to promote as an affiliate. Metrics can give you some great insight into what the customers are thinking when they see that product.

Metrics are not always going to be the same for your list as they are for someone else's list. They can be deceiving. Honestly, an offer that converts well in other sales funnels might not convert as well in your funnel.

As a broad example, if you're in the real estate niche and you try to promote a self-help or nutrition product, that product may convert really well, have a high EPC, and have a high Total Dollar per sale. However, it's more likely that it may not convert at all for your list because the people on your list are not used to seeing those offers from you, and they also might not even be interested in those types of offers.

So it's really important you understand that metrics don't always mean everything to everybody. While the above example is quite broad, if you have an offer that's closely related to your niche – and people in a similar market as you are promoting the product – you can deduce that you will have similar metrics or expect similar conversion numbers.

The most important thing to look for when choosing an offer is selecting one that people on your list *want* to see. If you can find an offer that people are craving for and want to see, that will always be an offer that will convert really well.

You should be a server to the wants and needs of the subscribers on your list. Having a better pulse on what types of services and products your list is looking for will undoubtedly explode your affiliate marketing business.

If it's an interesting product offer is useful to your list, you'll do a lot better than with just a general product with good metrics. In other words, make sure you're selecting affiliate offers that are relevant to your list.

In the beginning, you won't always know how your list will to respond to an offer. This is something that you will learn over time as you present more and more offers. Of course, you want to use your best guess when you were starting out and try to promote the best offers. You always want to listen to what your list is telling you. Pay attention to your conversion rates. Pay attention to your opt-out rates after you do a particular promotion via email.

If the subscribers on your list are buying a product that you offered, obviously they like the offer and are responding to it. If they are not buying it, then they clearly are not responding as well.

The best thing you can do for your own business is to look at metrics, understand them, and see what offers are converting well in the Internet marketing space in general. But more importantly, you want to take those metrics and look within your business and see if the offer is right for your list.

PUTTING TOGETHER AFFILIATE OFFERS

For the rest of this book, we're going to talk about choosing affiliate offers that go together or are synergistic to maximize the total dollar amount that you can sell to your list.

In putting together different affiliate offers, it's important to understand how to best incorporate them. Remember, your list is paying attention to what you are promoting and your offers have to make sense to your subscribers. If they get the feeling that you are out there just slinging products and not truly trying to add value to them in some way, it can turn them off pretty quick and result in less sales and possibly opt-outs. That's why having offers that go together and are complementary to one another is very important.

Why Have Other Offers?

Have a affiliate offers that go is good because you can tie them together in an autoresponder sequence and make more money than you would with just one affiliate product.

Another reason why you absolutely should have more than one offer in your autoresponder sequence and in your sequence to promote products to your list is because not every body on your list is going to respond to the offer that you think is the best to put in front of your list – even if it's your own product.

It's important to have multiple offers, because you need to keep in mind that every person that subscribes to your list has a cost associated with them. Now that cost can be time, meaning that you spent time in social media channels driving them to your email list. The cost can also be money, such as the money you spent on a lead generation campaign to build your funnel and build your list. The bottom line is you need to be able to monetize your subscribers. You have a business and ultimately you need to put quality offers in front of your list.

The reason to have additional offers is because not everyone will respond to the first, second, or even the third offer you put out there – not because your subscribers don't like you, but because people are just not going to buy everything you put in front of them. That's the simple truth. You want to put a variety of offers in front of your list so you can maximize the total dollar amount you are generating from your list.

Benefit: Sell More Affiliate Products

By putting more offers in front of your list, it will help you sell more affiliate products. The more products you sell, then the more money you make. It's obvious that, when you put multiple offers together, you're just going to sell more products. This will allow you to build your business much stronger and faster. That's what we are all striving for as affiliate marketers.

That's also why affiliate marketing is such an integral part on an online business, even if you are an information marketer or business owner. The reason why affiliate marketing is so beneficial to you is that it allows you to monetize your list anyways you would not otherwise generate any revenue.

For example, say everyone on your list is considered worth $5 each. If you can increase your average dollar per lead to $10, this means you can market more aggressively and you can generate much more sales – not only from the people that you have on your list now – it also allows you to spend more money and generate more leads to create a much bigger list. Why? Because you can now monetize new leads once they are in your list.

Benefit: Generate More Buyer Leads

The more offers that you put out there, the more buyers you're going to produce. It's that simple!

You can never have too many leads. Some leads are more valuable than others. But the most valuable leave that you have or the most valuable people on your list are your buyers. Obviously, you'd like them to be higher price-point buyers – the higher the price point of that buyer, the more valuable is that buyer. But ultimately, a buyer lead *always* is much more valuable than an opt-in lead.

Once someone from your list goes from an opt-in lead to a buyer, that subscriber is so much more valuable to you and your list. That person has recognized and responded to you, and have put their money where their mouth is – they pulled out their credit card! That's when your subscriber is truly important to you.

When you put multiple offers that go together in front of your list as part of an autoresponder sequence, you are going to generate more sales.

Benefit: Build a Better Rapport with Your List by Providing Good Products and Services

As long as you provide your list with valuable products and services that they would be interested in, it will actually increase their level of trust in you.

I realize that may sound counterintuitive. Many people who were starting out in this business get scared away of selling and promoting. But the bottom line is, if you have products that you believe in, products that you want to promote and will be of value to your list, it gives your list the opportunity to respond to you. I know it sounds funny, but the more that you promote to your list, especially when you're starting out, the more they become accustomed to you promoting products and services. This way they become less turned off when you do promote a product or service.

Many people make the mistake of trying to build a list but never putting a promotional offer out there. So what happens when they finally put a promotional offer out there, their list is turned off. They are turned off because they never got accustomed to any sort of offer being promoted to them.

So putting multiple offers out to your list is very important, and it actually make sure list better to your offers, because they are used to you putting out offers.

That's why when thinking about affiliate offers, don't think about just one offer. You're going to want to have multiple offers that you promote to your list.

As a side note, in this book we have talked exclusively about affiliate marketing. However, if you have and are selling your own product, this also applies. So if you see two affiliate offers that go together, take out the first affiliate offer and substitute it with your product. Then apply the same principle that the second product that is being sold as an affiliate product needs to be similar to your offer or complementary to your offer.

* * * * * *

For more information about Email Marketing and Affiliate Marketing, refer to the following books:

Book 4 – Affiliate Marketing 101
http://www.kippiperbooks.com/book4

Book 6 – Power of Email Marketing
http://www.kippiperbooks.com/book6

BONUS MATERIALS

Below is the link to this book's bonus material. I have developed this tools from my own experience as well as compiled from tools I have used from various training courses I have taken.

The mind map is built in XMind software. You can download a free version of XMind from http://www.xmind.net.

The item is also available as a PDF.

Strategic_Plan_Advanced_Affiliate_Marketing.xmind
http://www.kippiperbooks.com/make-money-online/book07/Strategic_Plan_Advanced_Affiliate_Marketing.xmind

Strategic_Plan_Advanced_Affiliate_Marketing.pdf
http://www.kippiperbooks.com/make-money-online/book07/Strategic_Plan_Advanced_Affiliate_Marketing.pdf

MORE KINDLE BOOKS BY KIP PIPER

Ultimate Affiliate Marketing with Blogging Quick Start Guide
http://www.kippiperbooks.com/UltimateGuide

Make Money Online Entrepreneur Series:

Below are just a few of the books in this series. To browse the entire series, go to:
http://www.kippiperbooks.com/makemoneyonlineseries

Book 1 – Freeing Up Your Time – VA's, Outsourcing & Goal Setting
http://www.kippiperbooks.com/book1
Book 2 – Your Core Business, Niche & Competitors
http://www.kippiperbooks.com/book2
Book 3 – Blogs & Emails: Your Link with Your Customers
http://www.kippiperbooks.com/book3
Book 4 – Affiliate Marketing 101
http://www.kippiperbooks.com/book4
Book 5 - Driving Traffic with Organic SEO
http://www.kippiperbooks.com/book5
Book 6 – Power of Email Marketing
http://www.kippiperbooks.com/book6
Book 7 – Quick Income Formula with Advanced Affiliate Marketing
http://www.kippiperbooks.com/book7
Book 8 – List Building with Facebook
http://www.kippiperbooks.com/book8
Book 9 – List Building with Twitter
http://www.kippiperbooks.com/book9
Book 10 - List Building with LinkedIn
http://www.kippiperbooks.com/book10

ONE LAST THING…

As you can probably tell from my writing, my intention is to inspire and support more people to build a better financial future. It's a tough economy today, and I think personal growth in the field of small business is more important than ever before. Even though I have well over 20 years of experience as a successful small business owner and online entrepreneur, I don't have all the answers. In fact I'm still learning myself, I just have my own opinions, experiences and a passion for being my own boss to guide me through life.

Thank you purchasing my eBook and for taking the time to read it. I hope you enjoyed it and found value within its pages.

If you did I would really appreciate your support by taking the time to write a review for me on Amazon. Reviews really help the authors you enjoy to get noticed in a crowded marketplace, and it would allow me to continue writing the books for this series and other business books.

Please visit the URL below to let me know your thoughts:

http://kippiperbooks.com/book7

All of my books are offered completely FREE on the launch and I want to reward loyal readers by offering my new books to them FREE of charge when they are released.

So please visit my website KipPiperBooks.com and either download your free copy of "28-Day Small Business Profit Plan: The Quick Start Guide to Business Success" or just sign up to my newsletter in order to be kept informed when the next release is due. I hate spam, so I promise I won't share your information with anyone – not for love nor money!

Good luck! I wish you every success in your personal and business endeavors.

www.ingramcontent.com/pod-product-compliance
Lightning Source LLC
Chambersburg PA
CBHW071412200326
41520CB00014B/3414